Michela

By United Library

https://campsite.bio/unitedlibrary

Table of Contents

Introduction

Michelangelo is one of the most famous and renowned artists in history.

He was an architect, poet, painter, sculptor, and even a musician. His work on the Sistine Chapel's ceiling is some of the most iconic art in the world.

Michelangelo Buonaroti (1475-1564), the great Italian sculptor and painter, was often called the greatest artist of all time due to his accomplishments during the Renaissance era. His work with the papacy included redesigning multiple churches and two grand commissions, including painting the ceiling of the Sistine Chapel for Pope Julius II.

Michelangelo wasn't just an artistic genius; he had a flair for verse and wrote hundreds of love sonnets and religious poems, some of which appeared in major publications such as The New Yorker Magazine. He also excelled at architecture and designed several buildings including one of his most celebrated works--St. Peter's Basilica in Rome.

Despite all his talents, Michelangelo had a tormented life as many people around him seemed to take advantage of his kindness and loyalty. Still, he remained unyielding and continued to create masterpieces for centuries to come; a true testament to his creativity and drive.

Michelangelo was not only a great artist but also a genius. He had a unique perspective on the world that allowed him to create some of the most beautiful and timeless pieces of art ever conceived.

Michelangelo

Michelangelo Buonarroti (Caprese, March 6, 1475 - Rome, February 18, 1564) was an Italian sculptor, painter, architect and poet.

A leading figure of the Italian Renaissance, even in his lifetime he was recognized by his contemporaries as one of the greatest artists of all time. A personality as brilliant as he was restless, his name is linked to some of the most majestic works of Western art, including the *David*, the *Moses*, the Vatican *Pietà*, the Dome of St. Peter's, and the cycle of frescoes in the Sistine Chapel, all of which are considered exceptional achievements of creative ingenuity.

The study of his works marked subsequent artistic generations by giving a strong impetus to the current of Mannerism.

Origins

Michelangelo Buonarroti was born on March 6, 1475, in Caprese, Valtiberina, near Arezzo, to Ludovico di Leonardo Buonarroti Simoni, podestà at the castle of Chiusi and Caprese, and Francesca di Neri del Miniato del Sera. The family was Florentine, but their father was in the town to hold the political office of podestà. Michelangelo was the second son, out of the couple's total of five children.

The Buonarroti of Florence were part of the Florentine patriciate. No one in the family had until then pursued a career in art, in the "mechanical" art (i.e., a craft requiring physical exertion) hardly in keeping with their status, holding instead positions in public offices: two centuries earlier an ancestor, Simone di Buonarrota, was on the Council of the Hundred Sages, and had held the highest public offices. They owned a shield of arms and patronized a chapel in the basilica of Santa Croce.

At the time of Michelangelo's birth, however, the family was going through a time of economic penury: his father was so impoverished that he was even about to lose his privileges as a Florentine citizen. The podesteria of Caprese, one of the least significant Florentine estates, was a political post of little importance, which he accepted to try to ensure a decent survival for his family by rounding out the meager income from some estates around Florence. The decline heavily influenced family choices as well as the young Michelangelo's fate and personality: concern for his and his family's economic well-being was a constant throughout his life.

Childhood (1475-1487)

As early as the end of March, when Ludovico Buonarroti's six-month tenure was over, he returned to Florence, to Settignano, probably to the then-named Villa Michelangelo, where the newborn child was entrusted to a local wet nurse. Settignano was a town of stonemasons, as pietra serena, which had been used in Florence for centuries in fine building, was quarried there. Michelangelo's wet nurse was also the daughter and wife of stonemasons. Having become a famous artist, Michelangelo, in explaining why he preferred sculpture to the other arts, recalled this very reliance, claiming that he came from a village of "sculptors and stonemasons," where from his wet-nurse he had drunk "milk mixed with marble dust."

In 1481 Michelangelo's mother died; he was only six years old. The boy's schooling was entrusted to the humanist Francesco Galatea da Urbino, who gave him grammar lessons. In those years he met his friend Francesco Granacci, who encouraged him in drawing. Cadet sons of patrician families were usually reserved for ecclesiastical or military careers, but Michelangelo, according to tradition, had manifested from a very young age a strong artistic inclination, which in Ascanio Condivi's biography, compiled with the collaboration of the artist himself, is recalled as having been hindered at all costs by his father, who did not, however, overcome his son's heroic resistance.

Training under Ghirlandaio (1487-1488)

In 1487 Michelangelo finally landed in the workshop of Domenico Ghirlandaio, one of the most highly regarded Florentine artists of the time.

Ascanio Condivi, in the *Life of Michelagnolo Buonarroti*, by omitting the news and emphasizing his father's resistance, seems to want to emphasize a more literary and celebratory motive, namely the artist's innate and self-taught character: after all, Michelangelo's willing start to a career considered "artisan" was for the custom of the time a ratification of the family's social demotion. That is why, once he became famous, he tried to conceal the beginnings of his workshop activity, speaking of it not as a normal professional apprenticeship, but as if it had been an unstoppable call of the spirit, a vocation, against which his father would have futilely tried to resist.

In fact, it now seems almost certain that Michelangelo was sent to the workshop by his own father because of family destitution: the family needed the money for the boy's apprenticeship, so he could not be given a classical education. The news is given by Vasari, who already in the first edition of the *Lives* (1550), described, in fact, how it was Ludovico himself who led his 12-year-old son to the workshop of Ghirlandaio, his acquaintance, showing him some sheets drawn by the boy, so that he could keep him with him, alleviating the expenses for the numerous children, and agreeing together with the master a "giusto et onesto salario, che in quel tempo si costumava". The same Arezzo historian recalls its documentary basis, in Ludovico's recollections and in the workshop receipts kept at the time by Ridolfo del Ghirlandaio, son of the famous painter. In particular, in a "recollection" of his father, dated April 1, 1488, Vasari read the terms of the agreement with the Ghirlandaio brothers, providing for a stay of the son in the workshop for three years, for a fee of twenty-five gold florins. Also on the art workshop's list of creditors, as of June 1487, 12-year-old Michelangelo is also recorded.

At that time Ghirlandaio's workshop was active at the fresco cycle of the Tornabuoni Chapel in Santa Maria Novella, where Michelangelo could certainly learn an advanced painting technique. The boy's young age (he was fifteen at the end of the frescoes) would relegate him to apprentice trades (preparing colors, filling simple and decorative scores), but it is also known that he was the best among his pupils and it cannot be ruled out that he was entrusted with some more important tasks: Vasari reported how Domenico had caught the boy "naturally portraying the bridge with some desks, with all the paraphernalia of art, et some of those young men working," so much so that he made the master exclaim, "Costui ne sa più di me." Some historians have speculated about his direct intervention in some of the ignudi of the *Baptism of Christ* and the *Presentation in the Temple* or in the sculptural *St. John in the Desert*, but in reality the lack of terms of comparison and objective findings has always made it impossible to definitively confirm.

What is certain, however, is that the young man showed a strong interest in the masters at the base of the Florentine school, especially Giotto and Masaccio, directly copying their frescoes in the chapels of Santa Croce and the Brancacci in Santa Maria del Carmine. One example is the massive *St. Peter by Masaccio*, a copy from the *Payment of Tribute*. Condivi also wrote of a copy from a German print of a *St. Anthony tormented by devils*: the work has recently been recognized in the *Torment of St. Anthony*, a copy from Martin Schongauer, purchased by the Kimbell Art Museum in Fort Worth, Texas.

To the Neoplatonic Garden (1488-1490)

Most likely Michelangelo did not finish the three-year training period in the workshop, judging from the vague indications in Condivi's biography. Perhaps he mocked his own master, replacing a portrait of Domenico's hand, which he had to remake for exercise, with his copy, without Ghirlandaio noticing the difference, "with a companion of his own [...] laughing about it."

In any case, it seems that at the suggestion of another apprentice, Francesco Granacci, Michelangelo began to frequent the garden of San Marco, a sort of art academy supported financially by Lorenzo the Magnificent on one of his properties in the Medici quarter of Florence. Here was a part of the Medici's vast collections of ancient sculpture, which young talents, eager to improve in the art of sculpting, could copy, supervised and helped by the old sculptor Bertoldo di Giovanni, a direct pupil of Donatello. Biographers of the time describe the garden as a true center of higher learning, perhaps emphasizing the everyday reality a bit, but it is without doubt that the experience had a fundamental impact on the young Michelangelo.

Among the various anecdotes related to the garden's activities, that of the *Faun's Head*, a lost marble copy of an ancient work, is famous in Michelangelo's literature. Seen by the Magnifico on a visit to the garden, it was good-naturedly criticized for the perfection of the teeth glimpsed through the open mouth, unlikely in an elderly figure. But before the gentleman had finished his tour of the garden, Buonarroti armed himself with a drill and hammer to chisel out one tooth and pierce another, prompting Lorenzo's surprised admiration. Apparently, following the episode Lorenzo himself asked permission from Ludovico Buonarroti to host the boy in the palace on Via Larga, his family's residence. Again sources speak of paternal resistance, but the onerous economic needs of the family had to play a determining role, in fact in the end Ludovico gave in exchange for a job at the customs office, paid eight scudi a month.

Around 1490 the young artist was then received as an adopted son into the most important family in the city. He thus became directly acquainted with the personalities of his time, such as Poliziano, Marsilio Ficino, and Pico della Mirandola, who made him a participant, to some extent, in neo-Platonic doctrine and the love of evoking the ancient. He also met the young scions of the Medici house, more or less his age, who became some of his main patrons in later years: Piero, Giovanni, later Pope Leo X, and Giulio, the future Clement VII.

Another fact related to those years is the quarrel with Pietro Torrigiano, a future sculptor of good standing, best known for his travels to Spain, from where he exported Renaissance manners. Pietro was known for his good looks and an ambition at least as great as Michelangelo's. There was bad blood between the two, and once they came into conflict during an inspection of the Brancacci Chapel, they ended up brawling; Michelangelo got the worst of it, cashing a punch from his rival right in the face, breaking his nose and having his profile disfigured forever. Following the brawl, Lorenzo De Medici exiled Pietro Torrigiano from Florence.

Early works (1490-1492)

To the period of the garden and stay in the Medici house date essentially two works, the *Madonna of the Staircase* (c. 1491) and the *Battle of the Centaurs*, both preserved in the Casa Buonarroti museum in Florence. These are two very different works in terms of theme (one sacred and one profane) and technique (one in a subtle bas-relief, the other in a bursting high relief), which testify to some fundamental influences in the young sculptor, respectively Donatello and classical statuary.

In the *Madonna of the Staircase,* the artist took up the technique of stiacciato, creating an image of such monumentality that it is reminiscent of classical stelae; the figure of the Madonna, which occupies the full height of the relief, stands out vigorously, amid notations of lively naturalness, as the Child is slumbering from behind and the putti, on the staircase from which the relief takes its name, occupied in the unusual activity of stretching a drape.

Slightly later is the *Battle of the Centaurs*, datable between 1491 and 1492: according to Condivi and Vasari it was executed for Lorenzo the Magnificent, on a subject proposed by Agnolo Poliziano, although the two biographers disagree on the exact titling.

For this relief Michelangelo drew on both Roman sarcophagi and Giovanni Pisano's pulpit panels, and he also looked to Bertoldo di Giovanni's contemporary bronze relief of a battle of horsemen, itself taken from a sarcophagus in the Camposanto in Pisa. In Michelangelo's relief, however, the dynamic tangle of struggling nude bodies is emphasized above all, and all spatial reference is nullified.

Michelangelo and Piero de' Medici (1492-1494)

In 1492 Lorenzo the Magnificent died. It is unclear whether his heirs, particularly his eldest son Piero, maintained their hospitality to the young Buonarroti: clues seem to indicate that Michelangelo suddenly found himself homeless, with a difficult return to his father's house. Piero di Lorenzo de' Medici, who also succeeded his father in the government of the city, is portrayed by Michelangelo's biographers as an "insolent and overbearing" tyrant, with a difficult relationship with the artist, who was only three years younger than him. Despite this, the documented facts leave no hint of a blatant break between the two, at least until the crisis in the fall of 1494.

In fact, in 1493 Piero, after being appointed a Worker in Santo Spirito, had to intercede with the Augustinian friars on behalf of the young artist, so that they would take him in and allow him to study anatomy in the rooms of the convent, dissecting corpses from the complex's hospital, an activity that greatly benefited his art.

During these years Michelangelo carved the *wooden Crucifix*, made as a thanksgiving for the prior. Also attributed to this period is the small *linden-wood Crucifix* recently acquired by the Italian state. Also, probably to thank or endear himself to Piero, he had to sculpt a lost *Hercules* soon after Lorenzo's death.

On January 20, 1494, a heavy snowfall hit Florence, and Piero called Michelangelo to make a snow statue in the courtyard of the Medici Palace. The artist again made a *Hercules,* which lasted at least eight days, enough for the entire city to appreciate the work. The work was perhaps inspired by Antonio del Pollaiolo for a small bronze now in the Frick Collection in New York.

As discontent grew over the gradual political and economic decline of the city, in the hands of a boy in his early twenties, the situation exploded on the occasion of the descent into Italy of the French army (1494) led by Charles VIII, toward whom Piero adopted an impudent policy of pandering, which he deemed excessive. As soon as the monarch left, the situation quickly precipitated, aided by the Ferrarese preacher Girolamo Savonarola, with the expulsion of the Medici and the sacking of the palace and garden of San Marco.

Realizing the impending political collapse of his patron, Michelangelo, like many artists of the time, embraced Savonarola's new spiritual and social values. The friar, with his heated sermons and formal rigorism, kindled in him both the conviction that the Church needed to be reformed and the first doubts about the ethical value to be placed on art, steering it toward sacred subjects.

Shortly before the situation precipitated, in October 1494, Michelangelo, in fear of becoming involved in the unrest as a possible target since he was protected by the Medici, secretly fled the city, abandoning Piero to his fate: in fact, on November 9 he was driven out of Florence, where a popular government was established.

The first trip to Bologna (1494-1495)

This was Michelangelo's first trip outside Florence, with an initial stop in Venice, where he stayed a short time, but enough to probably see Verrocchio's equestrian monument to Bartolomeo Colleoni, from whom he perhaps drew inspiration for the heroic and "terrible" faces.

He then headed to Bologna, where he was welcomed, finding hospitality and protection, by the nobleman Giovan Francesco Aldrovandi, who was very close to the Bentivoglio family that then ruled the city. During his Bologna sojourn, which lasted about a year, the artist took charge, thanks to the intercession of his patron, of the completion of the prestigious Ark of St. Dominic, on which Nicola Pisano and Niccolò dell'Arca, who had died a few months earlier that 1494, had already worked. He thus sculpted a *Saint Proculus*, an *Angel holding a candelabra*, and finished the *Saint Petronius* begun by Niccolò. These are figures that depart from the early fifteenth-century tradition of Niccolò dell'Arca's other statues, with an innovative solidity and compactness, as well as the first example of that Michelangelo-esque "terribleness" in the proud and heroic expression of the *St. Proculus*, in which an embryonic intuition seems sketched out that would develop into the famous David.

In Bologna, in fact, the artist's style had quickly matured through the discovery of new examples, different from the Florentine tradition, which deeply influenced him. He admired the reliefs of the Porta Magna of San Petronio by Jacopo della Quercia. From them he drew the effects of "restrained force," given by the contrasts between smooth, rounded parts and parts with rigid, fractured contours, as well as the choice of rustic, massive human subjects that enhance the scenes with sweeping gestures, eloquent poses and dynamic compositions. Even the same compositions of figures that tend to disregard the square edges of the panels and overflow with their compact masses and internal energy were a source of suggestion for the Florentine's future works, who in the scenes of the Sistine Vault will cite several times these scenes seen in his youth, both in the ensembles and in the details. Niccolò dell'Arca's sculptures must also have been subjected to analysis by the Florentine, such as the terracotta group of the Lamentation over the Dead Christ, where the face and arm of Jesus would shortly be recalled in the Vatican Pietà.

Moreover, Michelangelo was impressed by his encounter with Ferrara painting, particularly the works of Francesco del Cossa and Ercole de' Roberti, such as the monumental *Griffoni Polyptych*, the expressive frescoes in the Garganelli Chapel, or the *Pietà* by de' Roberti.

The Cupid Hoax (1495-1496)

Returning to Florence in December 1495, when the situation appeared to have calmed down, Michelangelo found a very different climate. A number of Medici had meanwhile returned to the city dominated by the Savonarola-inspired republican government. These were some members of the cadet branch who, for the occasion, took the name "Popolani" to endear themselves to the people, presenting themselves as protectors and guarantors of communal liberties. Prominent among them was Lorenzo di Pierfrancesco, great-cousin of the Magnifico, who had long been a key figure in the city's culture, a patron of Botticelli and other artists. It was he who took Michelangelo under his protection, commissioning two sculptures from him, both lost, a *St. John* and a *Sleeping Cupid*.

The *Cupid* in particular was at the center of an affair that soon led Michelangelo to Rome, in what can be said to be the last of his fundamental formative journeys. At the suggestion perhaps of Lorenzo himself and probably unbeknownst to Michelangelo, it was decided to bury the *Cupid*, to patina it as an archaeological find and resell it on the flourishing market for ancient works of art in Rome. The deception succeeded, in fact shortly thereafter, with the intermediation of the merchant

Baldassarre Del Milanese, the Cardinal of St. George Raffaele Riario, nephew of Sixtus IV and one of the richest collectors of the time, bought it for the conspicuous sum of two hundred ducats: Michelangelo had collected just thirty for the same work.

Soon after, however, rumors of the fruitful deception spread until they reached the ears of the cardinal, who, in order to get confirmation and demand his money back, sent one of his intermediaries, Jacopo Galli, to Florence, who traced it back to Michelangelo and was able to get confirmation of the fraud. The cardinal flew into a rage, but he also wanted to meet the artificer capable of emulating the ancients by having Galli send him to Rome in July of that year. With the latter, Michelangelo later formed a solid and fruitful relationship.

Arrival in Rome and the Bacchus (1496-1497)

Michelangelo accepted the cardinal's invitation to Rome without delay, despite the fact that the latter was a sworn enemy of the Medici: again out of convenience he turned his back on his protectors.

He arrived in Rome on June 25, 1496. That same day, the cardinal showed Michelangelo his collection of ancient sculptures and asked him if he felt up to doing something similar. Not even ten days later, the artist began sculpting a full-length statue of a *Bacchus* (now in the Bargello Museum), depicted as a teenager in the throes of intoxication, in which the impact with classical statuary is already legible: in fact, the work presents a naturalistic rendering of the body, with illusory and tactile effects similar to those of Hellenistic sculpture; unprecedented for the time is the expressiveness and elasticity of the forms, combined at the same time with an essential simplicity of detail. At the feet of Bacchus he sculpted a young man who is stealing a few grapes from the god's hand: this gesture aroused much admiration in all sculptors of the time since the young man really seems to be eating grapes with great realism. The Bacchus is one of Michelangelo's few perfectly finished works and from a technical point of view marks his entry into artistic maturity.

The work, possibly rejected by Cardinal Riario, remained in the house of Jacopo Galli, where Michelangelo lived. Cardinal Riario put his culture and collection at Michelangelo's disposal, thereby contributing greatly to the improvement of his style, but above all he introduced him to the cardinal's circle from which very important commissions would soon arrive. Yet once again Michelangelo showed ingratitude toward the patron of the day: about Riario he had his biographer Condivi write that he was ignorant and had commissioned nothing from him. Michelangelo was also said to be a magician.

Pieta (1497-1499)

Thanks again to Jacopo Galli's intermediation, Michelangelo received other important commissions in the ecclesiastical sphere, including perhaps the *Madonna of Manchester*, the painted panel of the *Deposition* for St. Augustine's, perhaps the lost painting of the *Stigmata of St. Francis* for San Pietro in Montorio, and, most importantly, a marble *Pietà* for the church of Santa Petronilla, now in St. Peter's.

This last work, which sealed Michelangelo's definitive consecration in the art of sculpture-at just twenty-two years of age-had been commissioned by the French cardinal Jean de Bilhères de La Groslaye, Charles VIII's ambassador to Pope Alexander VI, who perhaps wished to use it for his own burial. Contact between the two must have taken place in November 1497, following which the artist left for Carrara to select a suitable block of marble; the actual contract was not signed until August 1498. The group, highly innovative compared to the typically northern sculptural tradition of *Pietà*, was developed with a pyramidal composition, with the Virgin as the vertical axis and the dead body of Christ as the horizontal axis, mediated by the massive drapery. The finishing of the details was taken to extremes, so much so as to give the marble effects of translucence and waxy softness. Both protagonists show a young age, so much so that it seems the sculptor was inspired by the Dante passage "Virgin Mother, Daughter of your Son."

The *Pieta* was important in Michelangelo's artistic experience not only because it was his first masterpiece but also because it was the first work he did in Carrara marble, which from this moment on became the primary material for his creativity. In Carrara the artist manifested another aspect of personality: the awareness of his own talent. There, in fact, he purchased not only the marble block for the *Pieta*, but also several other blocks, in the belief that - given his talent - there would be no shortage of opportunities to use them. What was even more unusual for an artist of those times, Michelangelo became convinced that in order to sculpt his own statues he did not need clients: he could sculpt works on his own initiative to sell once they were finished. In practice, Michelangelo became his own entrepreneur and invested in his own talent without waiting for others to do it for him.

Passage to Siena (1501)

In 1501 Michelangelo decided to return to Florence. Before he left, Jacopo Galli got him a new commission, this time for Cardinal Francesco Todeschini Piccolomini, the future Pope Pius III. It involved making fifteen statues of *saints* slightly smaller than life-size for the Piccolomini altar in Siena Cathedral, architecturally composed some twenty years earlier by Andrea Bregno. In the end, the artist made only four of them (St. *Paul*, St. *Peter*, a *St. Pius* and *St. Gregory*), shipping them from Florence until 1504, moreover with heavy use of help. Indeed, the commission of the Sienese statues, intended for cramped niches, was now beginning to be too narrow for his reputation, especially in light of the prestigious opportunities that were looming in Florence.

Return to Florence: the *David* (1501)

By 1501 Michelangelo had returned to Florence, prompted by needs related to "domestic stores." His return coincided with the start of a season of prestigious commissions, testifying to the great reputation the artist had earned during his years in Rome.

For example, on August 16, 1501, the Opera del Duomo of Florence entrusted him with a colossal statue of *David* to be placed in one of the external buttresses placed in the apse area of the cathedral. This was an undertaking made complicated by the fact that the assigned block of marble had previously been rough-hewn by Agostino di Duccio in 1464 and by Antonio Rossellino in 1476, with the risk that portions of marble essential to the successful completion of the work had now been removed.

Despite the difficulty, Michelangelo began work on what was called "the Giant" in September 1501 and completed the work in three years. The artist approached the theme of the hero in an unusual way compared to the iconography given by tradition, depicting him as a young, naked man with a calm demeanor but ready for a reaction, almost symbolizing, according to many, the emerging republican political ideal, which saw the citizen-soldier-and not the mercenary-as the only one capable of defending republican freedoms. Florentines immediately recognized the statue as a masterpiece. Thus, even though the David was born for the Opera del Duomo and therefore to be observed from a lowered and certainly not frontal point of view, the Signoria decided to make it the symbol of the city and as such it was placed in the place with the greatest symbolic value: piazza della Signoria. Deciding on this placement of the statue was a specially appointed commission composed of the city's best artists, including Davide Ghirlandaio, Simone del Pollaiolo, Filippino Lippi, Sandro Botticelli, Antonio and Giuliano da Sangallo, Andrea Sansovino, Leonardo da Vinci, and Pietro Perugino.

Leonardo da Vinci, in particular, voted for a defiladed position for the *David*, under a niche in the Loggia della Signoria, confirming rumors of rivalry and bad relations between the two geniuses.

Concurrently with the placement of the David, Michelangelo may have been involved in the creation of the sculptural profile carved on the facade of the Palazzo Vecchio known as Michelangelo's L'Importuno. The hypothesis about Michelangelo's possible involvement in the creation of the profile is based on the latter's strong resemblance to a profile drawn by the artist, which can be dated to the early 16th century and is now in the Louvre. Moreover, the profile was probably carved with the permission of the city authorities, for the facade of the

Palazzo Vecchio was constantly manned by guards. So its author enjoyed a certain consideration and freedom of action. The strongly characterized style of the sculpted profile is close to that of the profiles of male heads drawn by Michelangelo in the early 16th century. Thus the sculptural portrait in the Palazzo Vecchio should also be dated to the early 16th century, its execution would coincide with the placement of the David, and it could perhaps represent one of the members of the aforementioned commission.

Leonardo and Michelangelo

Leonardo showed interest in the *David*, copying it in one of his drawings (although he could not share the work's marked muscularity), but Michelangelo was also influenced by Leonardo's art. In 1501 the maestro da Vinci exhibited in the Santissima Annunziata a cartoon of *St. Anne with the Virgin, Child and Little Lamb* (lost), which "made all the artisans marvel, but when it was finished, in the room lasted two days of going to see it the men and women, the young and the old." Michelangelo himself saw the cartoon, perhaps being impressed by the new pictorial ideas of atmospheric envelopment and spatial and psychological indeterminacy, and it is almost certain that he studied it, as shown by the drawings of those years, with more dynamic strokes, with greater animation of the outlines and with greater attention to the problem of the link between the figures, often resolved in dynamically articulated groups. The question of Leonardo's influence is a controversial topic among scholars, but some of them read traces of it in the two sculptural tondi he executed in the years immediately following. Widely acknowledged are undoubtedly two of Leonardo's stylistic innovations assumed and made their own in Michelangelo's style: the pyramidal construction of the human figures, which are large in relation to the natural backgrounds, and the "contrapposto," carried to the highest degree by Buonarroti, which makes dynamic the people whose limbs we see pushing in opposite spatial directions.

New Commissions (1502-1504)

The *David* kept Michelangelo busy until 1504, but did not prevent him from embarking on other projects, often of a public nature, such as the lost bronze David for a marshal of the King of France (1502), a *Madonna and Child* for Flemish cloth merchant Alexandre Mouscron for his family chapel in Bruges (1503), and a series of tondi. In about 1503-1505 he sculpted the *Pitti Tondo*, made in marble on commission from Bartolomeo Pitti and now in the Bargello Museum. Prominent in this sculpture is the different emphasis given to the subjects, from the barely sketched figure of John the Baptist (an early example of "unfinished"), to the fineness of the Virgin, whose head in high relief reaches out from the edge of the frame.

Between 1503 and 1504 he made a round painting for Agnolo Doni, representing the *Holy Family* with other figures. In it, the protagonists are grandly proportioned and dynamically articulated, against the background of a group of naked people. The colors are boldly vivid, ringing, and the sculpturally treated bodies had a dazzling effect on contemporary artists. Evident here is the clear and total departure from Leonardo's painting: for Michelangelo the best painting was that which most closely resembled sculpture, that is, that which possessed the highest possible degree of plasticity, and, after the unfinished oil tests that we can see in London, he will produce here an example of innovative painting, albeit with the traditional technique of tempera spread with dense cross-hatching. Curious is the affair related to the payment of the work: after the delivery the Doni, a very economical merchant, estimated the work a "discounted" amount compared to the agreed upon, infuriating the artist, who took the panel back, demanding, if anything, double the agreed price. The merchant had no choice but to pay without hesitation in order to obtain the painting. Beyond the anecdotal value of the episode, it can be counted among the very first examples (if not the first ever) of the artist's rebellion against the patron, according to the then absolutely new concept of the superiority of the artist-creator over the public (and thus the patron).

Finally, from c. 1504-1506 is the marble *Tondo Taddei*, commissioned by Taddeo Taddei and now in the Royal Academy of Arts, London: this is a work of more uncertain attribution, where, however, the unfinished effect stands out, present in the irregular treatment of the background from which the figures seem to emerge, perhaps an homage to Leonardo's spatial indefiniteness and atmospheric envelopment.

The Apostles for the Cathedral (1503)

On April 24, 1503, Michelangelo also received a commitment with the consuls of the Florentine Wool Art to produce twelve life-size marble statues of the Apostles, intended to decorate the niches in the pillars supporting the dome of the Florentine cathedral, to be completed at the rate of one per year.

The contract could not be honored due to various vicissitudes, and the artist only had time to rough out a *St. Matthew*, one of the earliest, conspicuous examples of unfinished work.

The Battle of Cascina (1504)

Between August and September 1504, he was commissioned to paint a monumental fresco for the Sala Grande del Consiglio in the Palazzo Vecchio that was to decorate one of the walls, more than seven meters high. The work was to celebrate Florentine victories, in particular the episode of the *Battle of Cascina*, won against the Pisans in 1364, which was to be a *pendant to* the *Battle of Anghiari* painted by Leonardo on the nearby wall.

Michelangelo only had time to make the cartoon, which was suspended in 1505 when he left for Rome and resumed the following year, in 1506, before being lost; it immediately became an obligatory study tool for contemporaries, and its memory is passed on both by autograph studies and copies by other artists. Rather than on the battle itself, the painting focused on the anatomical study of the numerous "naked" figures, caught in poses of considerable physical exertion.

The bridge over the Golden Horn (c. 1504)

As reported by Ascanio Condivi, between 1504 and 1506 the Sultan of Constantinople is said to have proposed to the artist, whose fame was already beginning to transcend national borders, to take charge of the design of a bridge across the Golden Horn, between Istanbul and Pera. Apparently, the artist had even prepared a model for the colossal undertaking, and some letters confirm the hypothesis of a trip to the Ottoman capital.

This would be the first hint of a willingness to embark on a major architectural project, many years before his official debut in this art with the facade for San Lorenzo in Florence.

The design for the drum of Santa Maria del Fiore (1507)

In the summer of 1507 Michelangelo was instructed by the Operai di Santa Maria del Fiore to submit, by the end of August, a drawing or model for the competition relating to the completion of Brunelleschi's dome drum.According to Giuseppe Marchini, Michelangelo is said to have sent some drawings to a woodworker for the construction of the model, which the same scholar recognized in the one identified with number 143 in the series preserved at the Museo dell'Opera del Duomo. This one presents an essentially philological approach, aimed at maintaining a certain continuity with the pre-existing one, through the insertion of a series of rectangular mirrors in green marble from Prato aligned with the capitals of the corner pilasters; a high entablature was planned, closed by a cornice with shapes similar to that of Palazzo Strozzi.However, this model was not accepted by the judging commission, which later approved Baccio d'Agnolo's design; the project included a massive gallery at the top, but work was halted in 1515, both because of the lack of favor it received and because of opposition from Michelangelo, who, according to Vasari, called Baccio d'Agnolo's work a *cricket cage.*

Around 1516 Michelangelo made some drawings (preserved at Casa Buonarroti) and probably had a new wooden model built, identified, albeit with wide reservations, with number 144 in the inventory of the Museo dell'Opera di Santa Maria del Fiore. Once again the abolition of the gallery is recorded, in favor of a greater prominence of the load-bearing elements; in particular, one drawing shows the insertion of tall free-standing twin columns at the corners of the octagon, topped by a series of strongly projecting cornices (an idea that would later be elaborated also for the dome of St. Peter's Basilica in the Vatican). Michelangelo's ideas were not actualized, however.

The tomb of Julius II, first project (1505)

It was probably Giuliano da Sangallo who told Pope Julius II Della Rovere, elected in 1503, about Michelangelo's astonishing Florentine successes. Indeed, Pope Julius had devoted himself to an ambitious program of government that firmly intertwined politics and art, surrounding himself with the greatest living artists (including Bramante and, later, Raphael) in the goal of restoring Rome and its authority to the grandeur of the imperial past.

Called to Rome in March 1505, Michelangelo was given the task of creating a monumental tomb for the pope, to be placed in the tribune (nearing completion) of St. Peter's Basilica. Artist and client agreed in a relatively short time (just two months) on the design and the fee, allowing Michelangelo, having collected a substantial down payment, to head immediately to Carrara to personally select the marble blocks to be carved.

The first design, known through sources, envisioned a colossal architectural structure isolated in space, with some 40 statues, scaled larger than life-size, on all four facades of the architecture.

The work of choosing and extracting the blocks took eight months, from May to December 1505.

According to the faithful biographer Ascanio Condivi, at that time Michelangelo thought of a grandiose project, to sculpt a colossus in the mountain itself, which could guide sailors: dreams of such unattainable grandeur were after all part of the artist's personality and are not believed to be a figment of the biographer's imagination, not least because of the existence of an edition of the manuscript with notes jotted down in dictation by Michelangelo himself (in which the work is described as "a madness," but one that the artist would have realized had he been able to live longer). In his imagination Michelangelo dreamed of emulating the ancients with designs that would have recalled such wonders as the Colossus of Rhodes or the giant statue of Alexander the Great that Dinocrates, mentioned in Vitruvius, would have liked to model in Mount Athos.

Rupture and reconciliation with the pope (1505-1508)

During his absence a kind of plot against Michelangelo was set in motion in Rome, prompted by envy among the artists in the papal circle. Indeed, the trail of popularity that had anticipated the Florentine sculptor's arrival in Rome must have made him immediately unpopular among the artists in the service of Julius II, threatening the pontiff's favor and the relative disposition of funds, which, though immense, were not infinite. It seems that it was in particular Bramante, the court architect in charge of initiating - a few months after the contract for the tomb was signed - the grandiose project for the renovation of the Constantinian basilica, who turned the pope's attention away from the burial project, which was judged to be a bad omen for someone still alive and in the midst of ambitious projects.

So it was that in the spring of 1506 Michelangelo, as he returned to Rome laden with marble and expectation after the grueling months of work in the quarries, made the bitter discovery that his mammoth project was no longer the focus of the pope's interests, shelved in favor of the basilica undertaking and new war plans against Perugia and Bologna.

Buonarroti asked in vain for a clarifying audience to get confirmation of the commission but, failing to be received as well as feeling threatened (he wrote "s'i' stare a Roma penso che fussi fatta prima la sepoltura mia, che quella del papa"), he fled Rome indignantly and in a hurry on April 18, 1506. Of no use were the five papal couriers sent to dissuade him and turn back, who pursued him, reaching him in Poggibonsi. Holed up in his beloved and protective Florence, he resumed some interrupted works, such as the *St. Matthew* and the *Battle of Cascina*. It took no less than three briefs from the pope sent to the Signoria of Florence and the constant insistence of Gonfaloniere Pier Soderini ("We do not wish for you to make war with the pope and put our state at risk") for Michelangelo to finally consider reconciliation. The occasion was given by the pope's presence in Bologna, where he had defeated the Bentivoglios: here the artist reached the pontiff on November 21, 1506, and in a meeting inside the Palazzo D'Accursio, narrated in colorful tones by Condivi, he obtained the commission to cast a bronze sculpture representing the pontiff himself full-length, seated and in large size, to be placed above Jacopo della Quercia's Porta Magna on the facade of the civic basilica of San Petronio.

The artist then stayed in Bologna for the time necessary for the undertaking, about two years. In July 1507 the casting took place, and on February 21, 1508 the work was discovered and installed, but it did not have a long life. Unloved because of the pope-conqueror's expression, more threatening than benevolent, it was brought down on a night in 1511, during the overthrow from the city and the temporary return of the Bentivoglio family. The wreckage, nearly five tons of metal, was sent to the Duke of Ferrara Alfonso d'Este, the pope's rival, who melted it down into a bombard, christened *the Giulia* in mockery, while the bronze head was stored in a closet. We can get a semblance of what this Michelangelo bronze must have looked like by looking at the sculpture of Gregory XIII, still preserved on the portal of the nearby Palazzo Comunale, forged by Alessandro Menganti in 1580.

The vault of the Sistine Chapel (1508-1512)

Relations with Julius II remained always stormy, however, because of the strong temperament they shared, irascible and proud, but also extremely ambitious. By March 1508 the artist felt himself released from his obligations to the pontiff, renting a house in Florence and devoting himself to suspended projects, particularly that of the *Apostles* for the cathedral. In April Pier Soderini expressed his desire to entrust him with a sculpture of *Hercules and Cacus*. On May 10, however, a papal brief reached him enjoining him to report to the papal court.

Immediately Julius II decided to occupy the artist with a new, prestigious undertaking, the redecoration of the vault of the Sistine Chapel. Due to the settling process of the walls, a crack had in fact opened in the ceiling of the chapel in May 1504, rendering it unusable for many months; reinforced with chains placed in the room above by Bramante, the vault needed to be repainted, however. The undertaking proved to be of colossal proportions and extremely complex, but it would give Michelangelo an opportunity to demonstrate his ability to overcome limitations in an art such as painting, which all in all he did not feel was his own and was not congenial to him. On May 8 of that year, therefore, the commission was accepted and formalized.

As with the tomb project, the Sistine undertaking was marked by intrigue and envy against Michelangelo, which is documented in a letter from Florentine carpenter and master builder Piero Rosselli sent to Michelangelo on May 10, 1506. In it, Rosselli tells of a dinner served in the Vatican rooms a few days earlier, which he had attended. The pope on that occasion had confided to Bramante his intention of entrusting Michelangelo with the repainting of the vault, but the Urbino architect had responded by raising doubts about the real abilities of the Florentine, who was poorly versed in fresco painting.

The contract for the first design included twelve apostles in the corbels, and partitions with geometric decoration in the central field. Two drawings by Michelangelo remain from this project, one in the British Museum and one in Detroit.

Dissatisfied, the artist obtained permission to expand the iconographic program, telling the story of humanity "ante legem," that is, before God sent the Tablets of the Law: in place of the Apostles he placed seven *Prophets* and five *Sibyls*, seated on thrones flanked by pillars supporting the cornice; the latter delimits the central space, divided into nine compartments through the continuation of the architectural members at the sides of thrones; in these compartments episodes taken from *Genesis* are depicted, arranged in chronological order starting from the altar wall: *Separation of Light from Darkness, Creation of the*

Stars and Plants, *Separation of the Earth from the Waters*, *Creation of Adam*, *Creation of Eve*, *Original Sin and Expulsion from the Earthly Paradise*, *Noah's Sacrifice*, *Universal Flood*, *Noah's Drunkenness*; in the five compartments surmounting the thrones the space narrows, leaving room for *Ignudi* holding garlands with oak leaves, an allusion to the pope's lineage i.e. Della Rovere, and bronze medallions with scenes from the Old Testament; in the lunettes and sails are the forty generations of *Christ's Ancestors*, taken from Matthew's Gospel; finally, in the corner pendentives are four biblical scenes, referring to as many miraculous events in favor of the chosen people: *Judith and Holofernes*, *David and Goliath*, *Punishment of Aman*, and the *Bronze Serpent*. The whole is organized in a complex decorative party, revealing his undoubted skills in architecture as well, which were destined to be fully revealed in the last decades of his activity.

The overall theme of the vault frescoes is the mystery of God's Creation, which reaches its climax in the realization of man in his image and likeness. With the incarnation of Christ, in addition to redeeming humanity from original sin, the perfect and ultimate fulfillment of divine creation is achieved, raising man even higher toward God. In this sense, Michelangelo's celebration of the beauty of the naked human body appears clearer. In addition, the vault celebrates the concordance between the Old and New Testaments, where the former prefigures the latter, and the prediction of Christ's coming in Jewish (with the prophets) and pagan (with the sibyls) circles.

Mounting the scaffold, Michelangelo began painting the three Noah stories crammed with characters. The work, exhausting in itself, was aggravated by the artist's typical self-satisfaction, delays in payment of fees, and constant requests for help from family members. In later scenes the depiction gradually became more essential and monumental: the *Original Sin and Expulsion from the Earthly Paradise* and the *Creation of Eve* show more massive bodies and simple but rhetorical gestures; after an interruption in the work, and viewing the vault from below as a whole and without the scaffolding, Michelangelo's style changed, accentuating more the grandiosity and essentiality of the images, even to the point of making the scene occupied by a single grandiose figure by nullifying all reference to the surrounding landscape, as in the *Separation of Light from Darkness.* In the vault as a whole these stylistic variations are not noticeable, indeed seen from below the frescoes have a perfectly unified appearance, given also by the use of a single, violent color scheme, recently brought to light by the restoration completed in 1994.

Ultimately, the difficult challenge on an undertaking of colossal dimensions and with a technique not congenial to him, with direct comparison with the great Florentine masters under whom he had trained (starting with

Ghirlandaio), could be said to have been fully successful beyond all expectations. The extraordinary fresco was inaugurated on All Saints' Eve 1512. A few months later Julius II died.

The second and third designs for the tomb of Julius II (1513-1516)

In February 1513, with the death of the pope, the heirs decided to resume the monumental tomb project, with a new design and a new contract in May of that year. One can imagine Michelangelo eager to take up the chisel again, after four years of exhausting work in an art that was not his favorite. The most substantial change to the new monument was the leaning against a wall and the elimination of the mortuary, features that were retained until the final design. The abandonment of the isolated monument, which was too grandiose and costly for the heirs, resulted in a greater crowding of statues on the visible faces. For example, the four seated figures, instead of being arranged on the two faces, were now planned near the two protruding corners on the front. The lower area had a similar score, but without the central portal, replaced by a smooth band highlighting the upward progression. The lateral development was still substantial, as the catafalque in a position perpendicular to the wall, on which the statue of the lying pope was supported, by two winged figures, was still provided. In the lower register, on the other hand, there still remained space on each side for two niches that repeated the pattern of the front elevation. Higher up, under a short rounded vault supported by pillars, was a *Madonna and Child* within a mandorla and five other figures.

Among the contractual stipulations was one that bound the artist, at least on paper, to work exclusively on the papal burial, with a maximum term of seven years for completion.

The sculptor set to work at a good pace and although he did not comply with the exclusive clause so as not to preclude himself from further extra income (such as by sculpting the *first Christ of Minerva*, in 1514), he made the two *Prisons* now in the Louvre (*Dying Slave* and *Rebel Slave*) and the *Moses*, which was later reused in the final version of the tomb. Work was often interrupted for trips to the Carrara quarries.

In July 1516 a new contract was reached for a third project, which reduced the number of statues. The sides were shortened and the monument was thus taking on the appearance of a monumental facade, moved by sculptural decoration. Instead of the smooth score in the center of the facade (where the door was located) a bronze relief was perhaps planned, and in the upper register the catafalque was replaced by a figure of the pope supported as in a *Pietà* by two seated figures, crowned by a *Madonna and Child* under a niche. Work on the tomb was abruptly interrupted by Leo X's commissioning of work on the basilica of San Lorenzo.

Michelangelo and Sebastiano del Piombo

In those same years, an increasingly heated competition with the dominant artist of the papal court, Raphael, led him to form a partnership with another talented painter, the Venetian Sebastiano del Piombo. Busy with other assignments, Michelangelo often provided drawings and cartoons to his colleague, who transformed them into paintings. Among these was, for example, the *Pietà* of Viterbo.

In 1516, a competition arose between Sebastiano and Raphael, sparked by a double commission from Cardinal Julius de' Medici for two altarpieces destined for his headquarters in Narbonne, France. Michelangelo offered conspicuous help to Sebastiano, drawing the figure of the Savior and the miracle worker in the canvas of the *Resurrection of Lazarus* (now in the National Gallery in London). Raphael's work, on the other hand, the *Transfiguration* was not completed until after the artist's death in 1520.

The facade of San Lorenzo (1516-1519)

Meanwhile, Lorenzo the Magnificent's son Giovanni had ascended to the papal throne under the name Leo X, and the city of Florence had returned to the Medici in 1511, entailing the end of the republican government with some apprehensions in particular for Michelangelo's relatives, who had lost political appointments and their associated compensation. Michelangelo worked for the new pope as early as 1514, when he redid the facade of his chapel at Castel Sant'Angelo (from November, a lost work); in 1515 the Buonarroti family was granted the title of conti palatini by the pope.

On the occasion of a trip of the pope to Florence in 1516, the facade of the Medici's "family" church, San Lorenzo, had been covered with ephemeral apparatus made by Jacopo Sansovino and Andrea del Sarto. The pontiff then decided to hold a competition to create a real facade, in which Giuliano da Sangallo, Raphael, Andrea and Jacopo Sansovino participated, as well as Michelangelo himself, at the invitation of the pope. The victory went to the latter, who at the time was busy in Carrara and Pietrasanta choosing marbles for the tomb of Julius II. The contract is dated January 19, 1518.

Michelangelo's design, for which numerous drawings and as many as two wooden models were executed (one is at Casa Buonarroti to this day) envisioned a narthex structure with a rectangular elevation, perhaps inspired by models of classical architecture, punctuated by powerful membranes animated by marble and bronze statues and reliefs. This would have been a fundamental step in architecture toward a new conception of the façade, no longer based on the mere aggregation of individual elements, but articulated in a unified, dynamic, and highly plastic manner.

Work proceeded at a slow pace, however, because of the pope's choice to use cheaper marble from Seravezza, whose quarry was poorly connected to the sea, making it difficult to transport it by river to Florence. In September 1518 Michelangelo also came close to death from a marble column that, while being transported on a wagon, broke loose, striking a worker next to him deadly, an event that deeply upset him, as he recounted in a letter to Berto da Filicaia dated September 14, 1518. In Versilia Michelangelo created the road for transporting marble, which still exists today (although it was widened in 1567 by Cosimo I). The blocks were lowered from the Trambiserra quarry in Azzano, in front of Monte Altissimo, to Forte dei Marmi (a settlement that sprang up at that time) and from there embarked at sea and shipped to Florence via the Arno.

In March 1520 the contract was terminated, due to the difficulty of the undertaking and high costs. During that period Michelangelo worked on the *Prisons* for the tomb of Julius II, particularly the four unfinished ones now in the Accademia Gallery. He also probably sculpted the statue of the *Genius of Victory* in the Palazzo Vecchio and the new version of the *Risen Christ* for Metello Vari (a work brought to Rome in 1521), finished by his assistants and placed in the basilica of Santa Maria sopra Minerva. Among the commissions received and not completed is a consultation for Pier Soderini, for a chapel in the Roman church of San Silvestro in Capite (1518).

The New Sacristy (1520-1534)

The change in papal desires was caused by the tragic family events related to the death of the last direct heirs of the Medici dynasty: Giuliano Duke of Nemours in 1516 and, above all, Lorenzo Duke of Urbino in 1519. To worthily house the remains of the two cousins, as well as those of the *Magnificent* brothers Lorenzo and Giuliano, respectively the father and uncle of Leo X, the pope matured the idea of creating a monumental funeral chapel, the New Sacristy, to be housed in the San Lorenzo complex. The work was entrusted to Michelangelo even before the final cancellation of the commission for the facade; after all, the artist had shortly before, on October 20, 1519, offered to the pontiff to create a monumental burial for Dante in Santa Croce, thus expressing his readiness for new commissions. Leo's death suspended the project only briefly, as already in 1523 his cousin Julius was elected, who took the name Clement VII and confirmed to Michelangelo all assignments.

Michelangelo's first plan was for an isolated monument in the center of the hall but, following discussions with the patrons, he changed it by planning to place the tombs of the Captains leaning against the center of the side walls, and those of the Magnificents, both leaning against the back wall in front of the altar.

The work was begun in about 1525: the structure in plan was based on Brunelleschi's *Old Sacristy*, also in the church of San Lorenzo: square in plan and with a small sacellum that was also square. Thanks to the membranes, in pietra serena and giant order, the room acquires a tighter, more unified rhythm; by inserting a mezzanine between the walls and lunettes and opening architraved windows between them, it gives the room a powerful ascending sense concluded in the ancient-inspired coffered vault.

The tombs, which seem to be part of the wall, resume at the top the aedicules, which are inserted above the eight doors of the room, four real and four fake. The tombs of the two captains are composed of a curvilinear sarcophagus surmounted by two statues lying with the *Allegories of Time*: in Lorenzo's the *Twilight* and the *Dawn*, and in Giuliano's the *Night* and the *Day*. These are massive figures with powerful limbs that seem to weigh down on the sarcophagi almost breaking them and releasing the souls of the deceased, portrayed in the statues inserted above them. Inserted in a niche in the wall, the statues are not shot from life but idealized as they contemplate: Lorenzo in a pensive pose and Giuliano with a sudden jerk of the head. The statue placed on the altar with the *Medici Madonna* is a symbol of eternal life and is flanked by statues of *Saints Cosmas and Damian* (protectors of the Medici) executed to Buonarroti's design by Giovanni Angelo Montorsoli and Raffaello da Montelupo, respectively.

On the work, though not continuously, Michelangelo worked until 1534, leaving it unfinished: without the funerary monuments of the Magnifici, the sculptures of the *Rivers at* the base of the tombs of the Capitani and, perhaps, of frescoes in the lunettes. Still, it is an extraordinary example of the perfect symbiosis of sculpture and architecture.

In the meantime Michelangelo continued to receive other commissions, which he only executed to a small extent: in August 1521 he sent the *Christ of Minerva* to Rome; in 1522 a certain Frizzi commissioned him for a tomb in Bologna and Cardinal Fieschi asked him for a sculpted *Madonna*, both projects that were never executed; in 1523 he received new solicitations from the heirs of Julius II, notably Francesco Maria Della Rovere, and the same year he was unsuccessfully commissioned for a statue of Andrea Doria by the Genoese Senate, while Cardinal Grimani, patriarch of Aquileia, asked him for a painting or sculpture that was never executed. In 1524 Pope Clement commissioned him for the Biblioteca Medicea Laurenziana, work on which got off to a slow start, and a ciborium (1525) for the high altar of San Lorenzo, later replaced by the Tribuna delle reliquie; in 1526 came a dramatic break with the Della Rovere family over a new, simpler design for the tomb of Julius II, which was rejected. Other unanswered requests for tomb designs came to him from the Duke of Suessa and Barbazzi canon of San Petronio in Bologna.

The insurrection and siege (1527-1530)

A common motif in Michelangelo's biographical story is his ambiguous relationship with his patrons, which has repeatedly led to talk of the artist's ingratitude toward his patrons. With the Medici, too, his relationship was extremely ambiguous: although they were the ones who pushed him toward a career in art and procured him commissions of the highest prominence, his staunch republican faith led him to harbor feelings of hatred against them, seeing them as the main threat against the Florentine *libertas*.

So it was that in 1527, when news of the Sack of Rome and the extremely harsh snub inflicted on Pope Clement arrived in the city, the city of Florence rose up against its proxy, the hated Alessandro de' Medici, ousting him and establishing a new republican government. Michelangelo fully adhered to the new regime, with support far beyond the symbolic level. On August 22, 1528 he went into the service of the republican government, resuming the old commission of the *Hercules and Cacus* (stopped since 1508), which he proposed to change to a *Samson with two Philistines*. On January 10, 1529 he was appointed a member of the "Nine of Militia," dealing with new defensive plans, especially for the hill of San Miniato al Monte. On April 6 of that year he received the post of

"Governor General over the fortifications," in anticipation of the siege that the imperial forces were about to lay. He specially visited Pisa and Livorno in the exercise of his office, and also went to Ferrara to study its fortifications (here Alfonso I d'Este commissioned him to paint a *Leda and the Swan*, later lost), returning to Florence on September 9. Worried about the worsening situation, he fled to Venice on September 21, planning to move to France to the court of Francis I, who, however, had not yet made him any concrete offers. Here, however, he was first caught up with the Florentine government's ban on him declaring him a rebel on September 30. He then returned to his city on November 15, resuming the direction of the fortresses.

Drawings of fortifications remain from this period, created through a complicated dialectic of concave and convex forms that look like dynamic machines suited to offense and defense. With the arrival of the Imperials to threaten the city, he is credited with the idea of using the stalls of San Miniato al Monte as an outpost with which to cannonade on the enemy, protecting the bell tower from enemy buckshot with armor made of padded mattresses.

The forces on the ground for the besiegers were overwhelming, however, and with its desperate defense the city could do nothing but negotiate a treaty, some of which was later disregarded, that would avoid the destruction and looting that had befallen Rome a few years earlier. In the aftermath of the Medici's return to the city (August 12, 1530) Michelangelo, who knew that he had been severely compromised and therefore feared revenge, went into hiding roguishly and managed to flee the city (September 1530), taking shelter in Venice. Here he stayed briefly, beset by doubts about what to do next. During this brief period he stayed on the island of Giudecca to keep away from the glitzy life of the city environment, and legend has it that he presented a model for the Rialto bridge to Doge Andrea Gritti.

The Laurentian Medici Library (1530-1534)

Clement VII's forgiveness was not long in coming, however, provided that the artist immediately resumed work at San Lorenzo, where, in addition to the Sacristy, he had five years earlier added a project for a monumental library. It is clear how the pope was moved, more than by pity for the man, by the knowledge that he could not give up the only artist capable of shaping his dynasty's dreams of glory, despite his conflicted nature. In the early 1930s he also sculpted an *Apollino* for Baccio Valori, the fierce governor of Florence imposed by the pope.

The public library, annexed to the church of San Lorenzo, was entirely designed by Buonarroti: in the reading room he based himself on the model of Michelozzo's library in San Marco, eliminating the division into naves and creating a room with walls punctuated by windows surmounted by mezzanines between small pillars, all with pietra serena moldings. He also designed the wooden pews and perhaps the pattern of carved ceiling and floor with terracotta decorations, organized in the same scores. The masterpiece of the design is the vestibule, with a strong vertical momentum given by the twin columns encircling the tympanum portal and the aediculae on the walls.

It was not until 1558 that Michelangelo provided the clay model for the grand staircase, which he had designed in wood but made at the behest of Cosimo I de' Medici in pietra serena: the bold rectilinear and elliptical, concave and convex forms are referred to as an early anticipation of the Baroque style.

1531 was an intense year: he executed the cartoon of the *Noli me tangere*, continued work on the Sacristy and Liberia of San Lorenzo, and for the same church designed the Tribune of the Relics; In addition, he was asked, unsuccessfully, for a project by the Duke of Mantua, the design of a house by Baccio Valori, and a tomb for Cardinal Cybo; the labors also led him to a serious illness.

April 1532 saw the fourth contract for the tomb of Julius II, with only six statues. In that same year Michelangelo met the intelligent and beautiful Tommaso de' Cavalieri in Rome, with whom he became passionately attached, dedicating drawings and poetic compositions to him. For him he prepared, among other things, the drawings with the *Rape of Ganymede* and the *Fall of Phaeton*, which seem to anticipate, in their powerful composition and theme of the fatal fulfillment of fate, the *Last Judgment*. Very tense relations he had, however, with the papal cloakroom attendant and Master of the Chamber Pietro Giovanni Aliotti, future bishop of Forli, whom Michelangelo, considering him too meddlesome, called the Tantecose.

On September 22, 1533, he met with Clement VII in San Miniato al Tedesco and, according to tradition, on that occasion they first discussed painting a *Last Judgment* in the Sistine Chapel. The same year his father Ludovico died.

By 1534 Florentine assignments were proceeding more and more wearily, with an increasing reliance on aid.

The Last Judgment (1534-1541)

The artist did not approve of Duke Alexander's tyrannical political regime, so with the opportunity of new assignments in Rome, including work for the heirs of Julius II, he left Florence where he never set foot again, despite Cosimo I's endearing invitations in his old age.

Clement VII had commissioned him to decorate the back wall of the Sistine Chapel with the *Last Judgment*, but he did not get to see even the beginning of the work, because he died a few days after the artist's arrival in Rome. While the artist was resuming the Burial of Pope Julius, Paul III was elected to the papal throne, who not only confirmed the commission for the Last *Judgment* but also appointed Michelangelo as painter, sculptor and architect of the Vatican Palace.

Work on the Sistine could be started in late 1536 and continued until the fall of 1541. To free the artist from his duties to the Della Rovere heirs Paul III went so far as to issue a motu proprio on November 17, 1536. If until then the various interventions at the papal chapel had been coordinated and complementary, with the *Judgment* came the first destructive intervention, which sacrificed Perugino's altarpiece of the *Assumption*, the first two 15th-century stories of Jesus and Moses, and two lunettes painted by Michelangelo himself more than twenty years earlier.

At the center of the fresco is Christ the Judge with Our Lady nearby, who turns her gaze toward the elect; the latter form an ellipse that follows Christ's movements in a whirlwind of saints, patriarchs, and prophets. Unlike traditional representations, everything is chaos and movement, and not even the saints are exempt from the atmosphere of restlessness, expectation, if not fear and dismay that expressively involves the participants.

Iconographic licenses, such as halo-less saints, apterous angels, and the young and beardless Christ, may be allusions to the fact that before judgment every single man is equal. This fact, which could have been read as a generic appeal to Catholic Reformation circles, together with the nudity and unseemly pose of some of the figures (St. Catherine of Alexandria prone with St. Blaise behind her), triggered harsh judgments against the fresco from much of the curia. After the artist's death, and with the changed cultural climate due in part to the Council of Trent, it came to the point where the nudes had to be covered and the most unseemly parts modified.

An equestrian statue

In 1537, around February, the duke of Urbino Francesco Maria I Della Rovere asked him for a sketch for a horse possibly intended for an equestrian monument, which was reported completed on October 12. The artist, however, refused to send the design to the duke, as he was dissatisfied. We also learn from the correspondence that by early July Michelangelo had also designed him a salt cellar: the duke's precedence over Michelangelo's many unfinished commissions is surely related to the pendency of work on the tomb of Julius II, whose heir Francesco Maria was.

That same year in Rome he received honorary citizenship at the Capitol.

Capitol Square

Paul III, like his predecessors, was an enthusiastic patron of Michelangelo.

With the relocation to the Capitol of the equestrian statue of Marcus Aurelius, symbol of imperial authority and by extension of the continuity between imperial and papal Rome, the pope commissioned Michelangelo in 1538 to study the renovation of the square, the center of Roman civil administration since the Middle Ages and in a state of decay.

Taking into account the pre-existing buildings, the two existing buildings, already renovated in the 15th century by Rossellino, were maintained and transformed, consequently creating the square with a trapezoidal plan, with the Palazzo dei Senatori in the background, equipped with a double ramp staircase, and bordered on either side by two palaces: the Palazzo dei Conservatori and the so-called Palazzo Nuovo built ex novo, both converging toward the staircase leading to the Capitol. The buildings were characterized by a giant order of Corinthian pilasters on the facade, with massive cornices and architraves. On the ground floor of the side buildings the pillars of the giant order are flanked by columns forming an unusual architraved portico, in a very innovative overall design that programmatically eschews the use of the arch. The inner side of the portico, on the other hand, features honeycombed columns that were later widely used, The work was carried out long after the master's death, while the paving of the square was not done until the early twentieth century, using a print by Étienne Dupérac that shows what must have been the overall design envisioned by Michelangelo, according to a curvilinear grid inscribed in an ellipse with at its center the base with rounded corners for the statue of Marc'Aurelius, also designed by Michelangelo.

Around 1539 he perhaps began *Brutus* for Cardinal Niccolò Ridolfi, a work with political meanings related to Florentine outcasts.

The Crucifixion for Vittoria Colonna (1541)

From about 1537 Michelangelo had begun a vivid friendship with the Marchioness of Pescara Vittoria Colonna: she introduced him to the Viterbo circle of Cardinal Reginald Pole, frequented by, among others, Vittore Soranzo, Apollonio Merenda, Pietro Carnesecchi, Pietro Antonio Di Capua, Alvise Priuli and Countess Giulia Gonzaga.

In that cultural circle they aspired to a reform of the Catholic Church, both internally and vis-à-vis the rest of Christendom, to which it was to be reconciled. These theories influenced Michelangelo and other artists. Dating from that period is the *Crucifixion* made for Vittoria, dated 1541 and possibly lost or never painted. All we have left of this work are a few preparatory drawings of uncertain attribution, the most famous of which is undoubtedly the one in the British Museum, while good copies can be found in the co-cathedral of Santa Maria de La Redonda and at the Casa Buonarroti. In addition, there is a painted panel, the Crucifixion of Viterbo, traditionally attributed to Michelangelo, based on a will of a Viterbo count dated 1725, on display in the Museum of the Colle del Duomo in Viterbo, more reasonably attributable to Michelangelo's environment.

According to the plans, it depicted a young and sensual Christ, symbolizing an allusion to Catholic reformist theories that saw the sacrifice of Christ's blood as the only way to individual salvation, without intermediation by the Church and its representatives.

A similar pattern was also present in the so-called *Pietà for Vittoria Colonna*, from the same period, known from a drawing in Boston and some copies by pupils.

Thus in those years in Rome Michelangelo could count on his circle of friends and admirers, including in addition to Colonna, Tommaso de' Cavalieri and artists such as Tiberio Calcagni and Daniele da Volterra.

Pauline Chapel (1542-1550)

In 1542 the pope commissioned him to do what represents his last pictorial work, where by then an old man he worked for almost ten years at the same time as other commitments. The Farnese pope, jealous and annoyed that the place where Michelangelo's painterly celebration reached its highest levels was dedicated to the Della Rovere popes, entrusted him with the decoration of his private chapel in the Vatican, which was named after him (Cappella Paolina). Michelangelo created two frescoes, working alone with laborious patience, proceeding with small "days," dense with interruptions and repentances.

The first to be made, the *Conversion of Saul* (1542-1545), features a scene set in a stark, unreal landscape, with compact tangles of figures alternating with empty spaces and, in the center, the blinding light from God descending on Saul on the ground; the second, the *Martyrdom of St. Peter* (1545-1550), has a cross arranged diagonally so as to form the axis of a hypothetical circular space with the martyr's face in the center.

The work as a whole is characterized by dramatic tension and marked by a feeling of sadness, generally interpreted as an expression of Michelangelo's tormented religiosity and the feeling of deep pessimism that characterized the last period of his life.

The completion of work on the tomb of Julius II (1544-1545)

After the final arrangements of 1542, the tomb of Julius II was put in place in the church of San Pietro in Vincoli between 1544 and 1545 with the statues of *Moses*, *Leah* (*Active Life*) and *Rachel* (*Contemplative Life*) in the first order.

In the second order, beside the lying pontiff with the *Virgin and Child* above him are a *Sibyl* and a *Prophet*. This design is also affected by the influence of the Viterbo circle; Moses an enlightened man shocked by the vision of God is flanked by two modes of being, but also by two modes of salvation not necessarily in conflict with each other: the contemplative life is represented by *Rachel* who prays as if to save herself she uses only Faith, while the active life, represented by *Leah*, finds her salvation in working. The common interpretation of the artwork is that it is a kind of mediating position between the Reformation and Catholicism due essentially to her intense association with Vittoria Colonna and her *entourage*.

In 1544 he also designed the tomb of Francesco Bracci, nephew of Luigi del Riccio in whose house he had received care during a serious illness that had struck him in June. Because of that indisposition, in March he had refused Cosimo I de' Medici the execution of a bust. That same year they began work on the Capitol, planned in 1538.

Old Age (1546-1564)

The last decades of Michelangelo's life are characterized by a gradual abandonment of painting and even sculpture, which he now practiced only on the occasion of works of a private nature. Instead, numerous architectural and town-planning projects take shape, continuing along the path of breaking with the classical canon, although many of them were completed in later periods by other architects, who did not always respect his original design.

Farnese Palace (1546-1550)

In January 1546 Michelangelo fell ill, being treated at the home of Luigi del Riccio. On April 29, having recovered, he promised a bronze statue, a marble one, and a painting to Francis I of France, which, however, he failed to do.

With the death of Antonio da Sangallo the Younger in October 1546, Michelangelo was entrusted with the fabrications of Palazzo Farnese and St. Peter's Basilica, both left unfinished by the former.

Between 1547 and 1550, therefore, the artist designed the completion of the facade and courtyard of Palazzo Farnese: in the facade he varied, compared to Sangallo's design, some elements that give the whole a strong plastic and monumental connotation but at the same time dynamic and expressive. To achieve this he increased the height of the second floor, inserted a massive cornice, and surmounted the central window with a colossal coat of arms (the two on either side are later).

St. Peter's Basilica in the Vatican (1546-1564)

As for the Vatican basilica, the history of Michelangelo's project can be reconstructed from a number of site documents, letters, drawings, frescoes and testimonies of contemporaries, but several pieces of information are conflicting. In fact, Michelangelo never drew up a final plan for the basilica, preferring to proceed by parts. In any case, several prints were published soon after the Tuscan artist's death in an attempt to restore an overall view of the original design; Étienne Dupérac's engravings immediately established themselves as the most widely used and accepted.

Michelangelo apparently aspired to a return to Bramante's central plan, with a square inscribed in the Greek cross, rejecting both the Latin cross plan introduced by Raphael Sanzio and Sangallo's designs, which called for a central plan building preceded by an imposing forepart.

He demolished parts built by his predecessors and, compared to the perfect symmetry of Bramante's design, introduced a preferential axis in the construction, assuming a main facade screened by a portico composed of columns of giant order (not realized). For the massive wall structure, which was to run along the entire perimeter of the building, he devised a single giant order of Corinthian pilasters with an attic, while in the center of the construction he built a drum, with coupled columns (surely made by the artist), on which was raised the hemispherical ribbed dome concluded by a lantern (the dome was completed, with some differences from the presumed original model, by Giacomo Della Porta).

However, Michelangelo's conception was largely disrupted by Carlo Maderno, who in the early 17th century completed the basilica by adding a longitudinal nave and an imposing facade based on the thrust of the Counter-Reformation.

In 1547 Vittoria Colonna died, shortly after the death of his other friend Luigi del Riccio: these were very bitter losses for the artist. The following year, on January 9, 1548, his brother Giovansimone Buonarroti died. On August 27 the Rome City Council proposed that the artist be entrusted with the restoration of the Santa Maria Bridge. In 1549 Benedetto Varchi published in Florence "*Due lezzioni*," held on a sonnet by Michelangelo. In January 1551 some documents from Padua Cathedral hinted at a model by Michelangelo for the choir.

The *Pieta* series (c. 1550-1555)

From about 1550 he began to make the so-called *Pietà dell'Opera del Duomo* (from its present location in the Museo dell'Opera del Duomo in Florence), a work intended for his tomb and abandoned after the artist shattered, in an access of rage two or three years later, the left arm and leg of Christ, also breaking the Virgin's hand. It was later Tiberio Calcagni who reconstructed the arm and finished the Magdalene left by Buonarroti in the unfinished state: the group consisting of Christ supported by the Virgin, Magdalene and Nicodemus is arranged in a pyramidal fashion with the latter at the apex; the sculpture is left at varying degrees of finish with the figure of Christ at the most advanced stage. Nicodemus would be a self-portrait of Buonarroti, from whose body the figure of Christ seems to emerge: perhaps a reference to the psychological suffering that he, a deeply religious man, carried within himself in those years.

The *Rondanini Pietà* was defined in the inventory of all works found in his studio after his death as, "Un altro statua principiata per un Cristo et un altro figura di sopra, attaccate insieme, sbozzate e non finite."

Michelangelo in 1561 gave the sculpture to his servant Antonio del Francese, however, continuing to make changes to it until his death; the group consists of completed parts, such as Christ's right arm, and unfinished parts, such as the Savior's torso pressed against the body of the Virgin almost forming a whole. After Michelangelo's death, at an unspecified time, this sculpture was moved to the Rondanini Palace in Rome and borrowed its name from there. It is currently in the Castello Sforzesco, purchased in 1952 by the city of Milan from a private estate.

Biographies

In 1550 Giorgio Vasari's first edition of *Vite de' più eccellenti pittori, scultori e architettori (Lives of the most excellent painters, sculptors and architects)* came out, which contained a biography of Michelangelo, the first written by a living artist, in the concluding position of the work that celebrated the artist as the apex of that chain of great artisans that started from Cimabue and Giotto, reaching in his person the synthesis of perfect mastery of the arts (painting, sculpture and architecture) capable of not only rivaling but surpassing the mythical masters of antiquity.

Despite the celebratory and encomiastic premises, Michelangelo did not like the operation, because of its numerous incorrectnesses and especially because of an uncongenial version of the tormented affair of Julius II's tomb. The artist then in those years worked with one of his faithful collaborators, Ascanio Condivi, getting a new biography published that reported his version of events (1553). Vasari drew on this, as well as on his direct acquaintance with the artist in the last years of his life, for the second edition of the *Lives*, published in 1568.

These works fed the legend of the artist as a tormented and misunderstood genius, pushed beyond his limits by adverse conditions and the changing demands of patrons, but capable of creating titanic and unsurpassable works.

Never had it occurred until then that this legend was then formed while the person concerned was still alive. Despite this enviable position attained by Buonarroti in old age, the last years of his existence were anything but peaceful, animated by great inner tribulation and troubled reflections on faith, death, and salvation, which are also found in his works (such as the *Pietà*) and writings.

Other events of the 1950s

By 1550 Michelangelo had finished the frescoes at the Pauline Chapel, and by 1552 the Campidoglio had been completed. In that year the artist also provided the design for the staircase in the Belvedere courtyard at the Vatican. In sculpture he worked on the *Pieta*, and in literature he worked on his own biographies.

In 1554 Ignatius of Loyola declared that Michelangelo had agreed to design the new Gesù church in Rome, but the intention was not followed through. In 1555 the election of Marcellus II to the papal throne compromised the artist's presence at the head of the St. Peter's building site, but soon afterward Paul IV was elected, who confirmed him in the post, directing him especially to work on the dome. Also in '55, his brother Gismondo and Francesco Amadori known as the Urbino, who had served him for twenty-six years, died; a letter to Vasari from that year gives him instructions for the completion of the Laurentian Library shelter.

In September 1556 the approach of the Spanish army induced the artist to leave Rome and take shelter in Loreto. While stopping in Spoleto he was met by a papal appeal that forced him to turn back. The wooden model for the dome of St. Peter's dates from 1557, and in 1559 he made drawings for the basilica of San Giovanni Battista dei Fiorentini, as well as for the Sforza chapel in Santa Maria Maggiore and the staircase of the Biblioteca Medicea Laurenziana. Perhaps that year he also initiated the *Rondanini Pietà*.

Porta Pia in Rome (1560)

In 1560 he made a design for Catherine de' Medici for the tomb of Henry II. Also the same year he designed Giangiacomo de' Medici's tomb for Milan Cathedral, later executed by Leone Leoni.

Around 1560 he also designed the monumental Porta Pia, a true urban setting with the main front facing inward into the city. The portal with a curvilinear pediment interrupted and inserted into another triangular one is flanked by fluted pilasters, while on the wall septum on either side are two gabled windows, with as many blind mezzanines above them. From the point of view of architectural language, Michelangelo manifested such an experimental and unconventional spirit that it has been referred to as "anti-Classicism."

St. Mary of the Angels (1561)

By now an old man, Michelangelo designed in 1561 a renovation of the church of Santa Maria degli Angeli within the Baths of Diocletian and the adjacent convent of the Carthusian fathers, which had been started in 1562. The space of the church was obtained by an intervention that, from a masonry point of view, today could be called minimal, with a few new wall septa within the large vaulted space of the *tepidarium* of the baths, adding only a deep presbytery and demonstrating a modern and non-destructive attitude toward the archaeological remains.

The church has an unusual transverse development, taking advantage of three contiguous bays covered with cross vaulting, to which two square side chapels are added.

Consul of the Academy of the Arts of Drawing

On January 31, 1563, Cosimo I de' Medici founded, on the advice of Arezzo architect Giorgio Vasari, the Accademia e Compagnia dell'Arte del Disegno, of which Buonarroti himself was immediately elected consul. While the Compagnia was a kind of guild to which all artists working in Tuscany had to adhere, the Accademia, consisting only of the most eminent cultural figures of Cosimo's court, had purposes of protection and supervision over the entire artistic production of the Medici principality. This was Cosimo's last, appealing invitation to Michelangelo to return to Florence, but once again the artist declined: his deep-rooted republican faith was likely to make him incompatible with service to the new Florentine duke.

Death

Only a year after his appointment, on February 18, 1564, at almost 89 years of age, Michelangelo died in Rome, in his modest residence in Piazza Macel de' Corvi (destroyed when the monument to Victor Emmanuel II was created), assisted by Tommaso de' Cavalieri. It is said that up to three days earlier he had been working on the *Pietà Rondanini*. A few days earlier, on January 21, the Congregation of the Council of Trent had decided to have the "obscene" parts of the *Last Judgment* covered.

The inventory drawn up a few days after his death (February 19) records a few possessions, including the *Pietà*, two small sculptures whose fate is unknown (a *St. Peter* and a small *Christ carrying the cross*), ten cartoons, while the drawings and sketches were apparently burned shortly before his death by the master himself. In a chest is then found a conspicuous "little treasure," worthy of a prince, which no one would have imagined in such a poor home.

The solemn funeral services in Florence

The master's death was particularly keenly felt in Florence, as the city had failed to honor its greatest artist before his death, despite Cosimo's attempts. The recovery of his mortal remains and the celebration of solemn funeral services therefore became a top city priority.

Within days of his death, his nephew Lionardo Buonarroti arrived in Rome with the specific task of recovering the body and arranging its transportation, an undertaking perhaps magnified by Vasari's account in the second edition of the *Lives*: according to the Aretine historian, the Romans opposed his requests, wishing to inter the artist in St. Peter's Basilica, whereupon Lionardo allegedly purloined the body at night and in great secrecy before resuming his way to Florence.

As soon as it arrived in the Tuscan city (March 11, 1564), the coffin was taken to Santa Croce and inspected according to a complex ceremonial, established by the lieutenant of the Academy of the Arts of Drawing, Vincenzo Borghini. This was the first funeral act (March 12) which, however solemn, was soon surpassed by that of July 14, 1564 in San Lorenzo, sponsored by the ducal household and worthy more of a prince than an artist. The entire basilica was richly adorned with black drapery and with panels painted with episodes from his life; a monumental catafalque was arranged in the center, adorned with ephemeral paintings and sculptures with complex iconography. The funeral oration was written and read by Benedetto Varchi, who extolled "the praises, merits, life and works of the divine Michelangelo Buonarroti."

The burial finally took place in Santa Croce, in a monumental tomb designed by Giorgio Vasari, composed of three weeping figures representing painting, sculpture, and architecture.

The state funeral sealed the *status* achieved by the artist and was the final consecration of his legend as an unsurpassed creator, capable of reaching creative heights in any artistic field and, more than those of any other, able to emulate the act of divine creation.

Rime

Regarded by him as a "silly thing," his poetic activity is being characterized, in contrast to the usual sixteenth-century Petrarch-influenced activity, by energetic, austere and intensely expressive tones taken from Dante's poems.

The earliest poetic compositions date to the years 1504-1505, but it is likely that he made some earlier as well, since we know that many of his early manuscripts were lost.

His poetic training probably took place on the texts of Petrarch and Dante, known in the humanistic circle of Lorenzo de' Medici's court. His early sonnets are related to various themes connected with his artistic work, sometimes reaching the grotesque with bizarre images and metaphors. Next are the sonnets made for Vittoria Colonna and Tommaso de' Cavalieri; in them Michelangelo focuses more on the Neoplatonic theme of love, both divine and human, which is all played out around the contrast between love and death, resolving it with solutions that are now dramatic, now ironically detached.

In his later years his rhymes focus more on the theme of sin and individual salvation; here the tone becomes bitter and sometimes anguished, so much so that he realizes true mystical visions of the divine.

Michelangelo's rhymes met with some fortune in the United States in the nineteenth century after their translation by the great philosopher Ralph Waldo Emerson.

Michelangelo's sculptural technique

From a technical point of view, Michelangelo the sculptor, as, moreover, is often the case with genius artists, did not follow a creative process bound by fixed rules; but in principle, however, usual or more frequent principles can be traced.

First of all, Michelangelo was the first sculptor who, in stone, never attempted to color or gild certain parts of the statues; in fact, he preferred to color the enhancement of the "soft radiance" of the stone, often with chiaroscuro effects evident in the statues left without the last finish, with the chisel strokes enhancing the peculiarity of the marble material.

The only bronzes he executed are destroyed or lost (the *David De Rohan* and the *Blessing Julius II*); the paucity of his use of such material clearly shows how he disliked the "atmospheric" effects derived from modeling clay. He after all declared himself to be an artist "of the levare," rather than "of the mettere," that is, for him the final figure was born from a process of subtraction of the material down to the core of the sculptural subject, which was as it were already "imprisoned" in the marble block. In such finished material he found the calm brilliance of the smooth and clear surfaces, which were best suited to enhance the epidermis of the solid musculatures of his figures.

Preparatory studies

The technical procedure by which Michelangelo sculpted is known to us from some traces in studies and drawings and from a few testimonies. It seems that initially, following the custom of sixteenth-century sculptors, he prepared general and detailed studies in the form of sketches and studies. He then personally instructed the quarrymen with drawings (some of which still exist) that gave a precise idea of the block to be cut, with measurements in Florentine cubits, sometimes going so far as to outline the position of the statue within the block itself. Sometimes in addition to preparatory drawings he executed wax or clay models, fired or not, which are the subject of some evidence, albeit indirect, and some of which are still preserved today, although none is definitely documented. More rare, on the other hand, it seems, is the use of a model in its final dimensions, of which, however, the isolated testimony of the *River God* remains.

As the years went by, however, he had to thin out his preparatory studies in favor of an immediate attack on stone moved by urgent ideas, susceptible, however, to be profoundly changed in the course of the work (as in the *Rondanini Pietà*).

Block preparation

The first intervention on the block coming out of the quarry was with the "cagnaccia," which smoothed the smooth and geometric surfaces according to the idea to be realized. It seems that only after this first appropriation of the marble did Michelangelo trace on the surface made irregular a rudimentary mark with charcoal that highlighted the main (i.e., frontal) view of the work. The traditional technique was to use proportional squares or rectangles to bring the measurements of the models back to the final ones, but it is not certain that Michelangelo did this by eye. Another procedure in the early stages of sculpting was to transform the charcoal trace into a series of small holes to guide the lunge as the pencil mark disappeared.

Roughing

At this point the actual sculpting had begun, carving the marble starting from the main view, leaving the most prominent parts intact and gradually penetrating into the deeper layers. This was done with a mallet and a large pointed chisel, the subbia. There is a valuable account by B. de Vigenère, who saw the master, now over sixty, approach a block at this stage: despite Michelangelo's "not the sturdiest" appearance, he is remembered as knocking down "flakes of a very hard marble in a quarter of an hour," better than three young stonecutters could have done in three or four times as much time, and he pounced "on the marble with such impetuosity and fury, that I thought the whole work must have fallen to pieces. With a single blow he would take out flakes three or four fingers thick, and with such exactness to the mark drawn, that if he had blown off a tad more marble he ran the risk of ruining everything."

On the fact that the marble was to be "attacked" by the main view remains the testimony of Vasari and Cellini, two devotees of Michelangelo, who convincingly insist that the work was to be worked initially as if it were a relief, mocking the procedure of starting all sides of the block, later finding that the lateral and tergal views do not coincide with the frontal one, thus requiring "patches" with pieces of marble, according to a procedure that "is art by certain cobblers, who make it very badly." Certainly Michelangelo did not use "patches," but it cannot be excluded that during the development of the frontal view he did not neglect the secondary views, which were a direct consequence of it. Such a procedure is evident in some unfinished works, such as the famous *Prisoners* that seem to break free from stone.

Sculpting and leveling

After the subbia had removed a lot of material, they moved on to the deep search, which was done using toothed chisels: Vasari described two types, the calcagnuolo, stubby and equipped with one notch and two teeth, and the gradina, finer and equipped with two notches and three or more teeth. Judging from the surviving traces, Michelangelo must have preferred the second, by which the carving proceeds "throughout with gentleness, graduating the figure with the proportion of muscles and folds." These are those hatchings that are clearly visible in various Michelangelo works (think of the face of the Child in the *Pitti Tondo*), which often coexist alongside newly rough-hewn areas with subbia or the simpler initial personalizations of the block (as in the *St. Matthew*).

The next stage was leveling with a flat chisel, which removed the traces of the step (a stage in the middle of the work is seen in the *Day*), unless this was done with the step itself.

Finishing

It appears evident that the master, in his impatience to see the conceived forms palpitate, would move from one operation to another, implementing the different operational stages simultaneously. Remaining always evident the superior logic that coordinated the different parts, the quality of the work always appeared to be very high, even in the different levels of fineness, thus explaining how the master could interrupt the work when it was still "unfinished," even before the last phase, often prepared by aides, in which the statue was smoothed with scrapers, files, pumice stone and, finally, balls of straw. This final smoothing, present for example in the *Vatican Pietà* still ensured that extraordinary luster, which stood apart from the graininess of the works of the Tuscan masters of the 15th century.

Michelangelo's unfinished

One of the most difficult issues for critics in Michelangelo's albeit complex oeuvre is the knot of the unfinished. Indeed, the number of statues left unfinished by the artist is so great that the only causes are unlikely to be contingent factors outside the sculptor's control, making it somewhat likely that he had a direct will and a certain complacency for incompleteness.

Explanations proposed by scholars range from character factors (the artist's continuous loss of interest in commissions he had started) to artistic factors (the unfinished work as an additional expressive factor): here unfinished works appear to struggle against inert material to come to light, as in the famous case of the *Prisoners*, or they have blurred contours that differentiate spatial planes (as in the *Tondo Pitti*) or they become universal types, without clearly defined somatic characteristics, as in the case of the allegories in the Medici tombs.

Some have linked most of the unfinished works to periods of strong inner torment on the part of the artist, combined with constant dissatisfaction, which could have caused the works to be stopped prematurely. Others have dwelt on technical reasons, related to the artist's particular sculptural technique based on "levare" and almost always relying on the inspiration of the moment, always subject to variation. Thus, once arrived at within the block, at a form obtained by erasing away too much stone, it could happen that a change of idea was no longer possible at the stage reached, making the prerequisites for being able to continue the work (as in the *Rondanini Pietà*) lacking.

Personality

The legend of the genius artist has often cast a second light on the man in his entirety, endowed also with weaknesses and dark sides. These characteristics have been the subject of studies in recent years, which, by stripping away the divine aura of his figure, have laid bare a truer and more accurate portrait than that which emerges from ancient sources, less condescending but certainly more human.

Among the most obvious flaws in his personality were his short temper (some have gone so far as to speculate that he had Asperger's syndrome), touchiness, and constant dissatisfaction. Numerous contradictions animated his behavior, among which stood out for particular strength were his attitude toward money and his relations with his family, which were two intimately related aspects, however.

Both the correspondence and Michelangelo's *Memories* books make constant allusions to money and its scarcity, so much so that it would appear that the artist lived and died in absolute poverty. Rab Hatfield's studies of his bank deposits and possessions, however, have outlined a quite different situation, showing how during his existence he managed to accumulate immense wealth. The inventory drawn up in the mansion of Macel de' Corvi in the aftermath of his death suffices as an example: the initial part of the document seems to confirm his poverty, recording two beds, a few items of clothing, a few everyday objects, and a horse; but in his bedroom a locked casket is later found which, when opened, demonstrates a cash hoard worthy of a prince. By way of example with that cash the artist could very well have bought himself a palace, being a higher sum than that shelled out in those years (in 1549) by Eleonora di Toledo for the purchase of the Pitti Palace.

What emerges, then, is a figure who, although wealthy, lived in austerity by spending very sparingly and neglecting himself to unthinkable limits: Condivi recalls, for example, how he used not to take off his boots before going to bed, as the indigent did.

This pronounced avarice and greed, which continually made him perceive his own patrimony in a distorted way, were certainly due to character reasons, but also to more complex motivations related to his difficult relationship with his family. The painful economic situation of the Buonarroti family must have intimately scarred him, and perhaps he had as a desire to leave them a substantial inheritance to lift their fortunes. But this is apparently contradicted by his refusals to help his father and brothers, justifying himself with an imagined lack of liquidity, and on other occasions he went so far as to demand the return of sums lent in the past, accusing them of living off his labors, if not shamelessly taking advantage of his generosity.

Alleged homosexuality

Several historians have addressed the issue of Michelangelo's alleged homosexuality by examining verses dedicated to certain men (Febo Dal Poggio, Gherardo Perini, Cecchino Bracci, Tommaso de' Cavalieri). See, for example, the sonnet dedicated to Tommaso de' Cavalieri-written in 1534-in which Michelangelo denounced the people's habit of vocalizing about his love affairs:

On the drawing of the *Fall of Phaeton*, in the British Museum, Michelangelo wrote a dedication to Tommaso de' Cavalieri.

Many sonnets were also dedicated to Cecchino Bracci, whose tomb Michelangelo designed in the Basilica of Santa Maria in Aracoeli. On the occasion of Cecchino's untimely death, Buonarroti wrote an epitaph (first published only in 1960) with strong carnal ambiguity:

In fact, the epitaph says nothing about such an alleged relationship between the two. After all, Michelangelo's epitaphs were commissioned by Luigi Riccio and paid for by him through gastronomic gifts, while the acquaintance between Buonarroti and Bracci was only marginal.

The numerous epitaphs written by Michelangelo for Cecchino were published posthumously by his nephew, who, however, frightened by the homoerotic implications of the text, would change the sex of the addressee in several places, making him a woman. Later editions would take up the censored text, and only the Laterza edition of the *Rime*, in 1960, would restore the original diction.

However, the theme of the male nude in motion is central to all of Michelangelo's work, so much so that his aptitude for depicting even women with distinctly masculine features is famous (one example above all, the *Sibyls* of the Sistine Chapel vault). This is not conclusive evidence of homosexual attitudes, but it is undeniable that Michelangelo never portrayed a "Fornarina" or a "Violante" of his own; rather, the protagonists of his art are always vigorous masculine individuals.

In 1536 or 1538 is to be placed the first meeting with Vittoria Colonna. In 1539 she returned to Rome and there grew a friendship with Michelangelo, who loved her (at least from a Platonic point of view) enormously and over whom she had a great influence, probably also a religious one. To her the artist dedicated some of the most profound and powerful poems of his life.

Biographer Ascanio Condivi also recalled how the artist after the woman's death regretted that he had never kissed the widow's face in the same way he had shaken her hand.

Michelangelo never took a wife, and his love affairs with neither women nor men are documented. Late in life he devoted himself to intense and austere religiosity.

Sources on Michelangelo

Michelangelo is the artist who, perhaps more than any other, embodies the myth of a brilliant and versatile personality, capable of accomplishing titanic feats despite complex personal vicissitudes, suffering and torment due to the difficult historical moment of political, religious and cultural upheaval. A fame that has not faded over the centuries, remaining more alive than ever even in the present day.

If his ingenuity and talent have never been questioned, not even by his fiercest detractors, this alone is not enough to explain his legendary aura, nor are his restlessness, or the suffering and passion with which he participated in the events of his time sufficient: these are traits that, at least in part, can also be found in other artists who lived more or less in his era. Undoubtedly his myth also fed on himself, in the sense that Michelangelo was the first and most effective of its promoters, as is evident from the sources that are fundamental to reconstructing his biography and his artistic and personal affairs: the correspondence and the three biographies about him in his time.

The correspondence

During his lifetime Michelangelo wrote numerous letters, most of which have been preserved in archives and private collections, most notably the nucleus collected by his descendants in the Buonarroti household. Michelangelo's complete correspondence was published in 1965 and has been fully available online since 2014.

In his writings, the artist often describes his states of mind and vents the worries and torments that plagued him; moreover, in the epistolary exchange he often takes the opportunity to report his own version of events, especially when he finds himself accused or put in a bad light, as in the case of the numerous projects he started and then abandoned before completion. He often complains about principals who turn their backs on him and makes heavy accusations against those who hinder or contradict him. When he finds himself in trouble, as in the darkest moments of the struggle with the della Rovere heirs over the sepulchral monument to Julius II, the tone of his letters becomes more heated, always finding justification for his own conduct, carving out the part of innocent and misunderstood victim. One can go so far as to speak of a definite design, through the numerous letters, aimed at exonerating him of all blame and procuring for himself a heroic aura of great resistance to the travails of life.

The first edition of Vasari's *Lives* (1550)

In March 1550, Michelangelo, nearly 75 years old, saw himself published in a biography of himself in the volume of *Lives of the Most Excellent Painters, Sculptors and Architects* written by Arezzo artist and historian Giorgio Vasari and published by Florentine publisher Lorenzo Torrentino. The two had met briefly in Rome in 1543, but a sufficiently established relationship had not been established for the Aretine to question Michelangelo. It was the first biography of an artist composed while he was still alive, pointing to him as the culmination of a progression in Italian art from Cimabue, the first able to break with the "Greek" tradition, to him, the unsurpassed artificer able to rival the ancient masters.

Despite the praise, the artist did not approve of some errors, due to the lack of direct knowledge between the two, and especially of some reconstructions that, on hot topics such as the pope's burial, contradicted his version constructed in the correspondence. Vasari after all seems not to have sought out written documents, relying almost exclusively on friendships more or less close to Buonarroti, including Francesco Granacci and Giuliano Bugiardini, already his collaborators, who, however, exhausted their direct contacts with the artist shortly after work on the Sistine Chapel began, until about 1508.

If the part about the youth and twenties in Florence thus appears well documented, the Roman years are more vague, stopping however at 1547, the year in which the drafting had to be completed.

Among the errors that hurt Michelangelo most were misinformation about his stay with Julius II, with his flight from Rome being attributed to the time of the Sistine Chapel vault, due to a quarrel with the pope over his refusal to unveil the frescoes to him in advance.Vasari knew of the strong disagreements between the two but at the time completely ignored the causes, namely the dispute over the painful affair of the tomb.

The biography of Ascanio Condivi (1553)

It is no coincidence that just three years later, in 1553, a new biography of Michelangelo, by the Marche painter Ascanio Condivi, his disciple and collaborator, was printed. Condivi was a modest figure on the artistic scene, and even in the literary field, judging from certainly autograph writings such as his letters, he must have had little talent. The elegant prose of the *Life of Michelagnolo Buonarroti* is in fact assigned by critics to Annibale Caro, a prominent intellectual very close to the Farnese family, who had at least a guiding and revising role.

In terms of content, the person directly responsible must almost certainly have been Michelangelo himself, with a design of self-defense and personal celebration almost identical to that of the correspondence. The purpose of the literary enterprise was as expressed in the preface: in addition to setting an example for young artists, it was to "supplire al difetto di quelli, et prevenire l'ingiuria di questi altri," a clear reference to Vasari's errors.

Condivi's biography is thus not free from selective interventions and biased reconstructions. If it dwells much on his youthful years, it is silent, for example, on his apprenticeship at Ghirlandaio's workshop, in order to emphasize the impelling and self-taught character of the genius, opposed by his father and circumstances. More rapid is the review of the years of old age, while the hinge of the tale concerns the "tragedy of the burial," reconstructed in great detail and with a vividness that makes it one of the most interesting passages in the volume. The years immediately preceding the release of the biography were in fact those of the most difficult relations with the Della Rovere heirs, undermined by bitter confrontations and threats to denounce them to the public authorities and demand the advances paid, so it is easy to imagine how much it pressed the artist to provide his own version of the affair.

Another flaw in Condivi's biography is that, apart from rare exceptions such as the *St. Matthew* and the sculptures for the New Sacristy, it is silent on the many unfinished projects, as if as the years passed Buonarroti was now troubled by the memory of works left unfinished.

The second edition of Vasari's *Lives* (1568)

Four years after the artist's death and eighteen years after his first work, Giorgio Vasari published a new edition of the *Lives* for the publisher Giunti, revised, expanded and updated. That of Michelangelo in particular was the most revised biography and at the most anticipated by the public, so much so that it was also published in a separate booklet by the same publisher. Indeed, with his death, the legend of the artist had further increased, and Vasari, the protagonist of the funeral to Michelangelo held solemnly in Florence, did not hesitate to refer to him as the "divine" artist. Compared to the previous edition, it seems clear that in those years Vasari became better documented and had access to first-hand information, thanks to a strong direct link that had been established between the two.

The new account is thus much more complete and also verified by numerous written documents. The gaps were filled with his frequentation of the artist during the years of his work with Julius III (1550-1554) and with the appropriation of entire passages from Condivi's biography, a true literary "plundering": identical are some paragraphs and the conclusion, without some mention of the source, indeed the only mention of the Marche artist is to hold against him the omission of his apprenticeship at Ghirlandaio's workshop, a fact instead known from documents reported by Vasari himself.

The completeness of the second edition is a source of pride for the Aretine: "all that [...] that will be written at the present time is the truth, nor do I know of anyone who has practiced him more than I have, and who has been more of a faithful friend and servant to him, as he is witness to it up to those who do not know; nor do I believe that there is anyone who can show more letters written by him proper, nor with more affection than he has done to me."

The *Roman Dialogues* of Francisco de Hollanda

The work that has been considered by some historians to bear witness to Michelangelo's artistic ideas are the *Roman Dialogues* written by Francisco de Hollanda as a supplement to his treatise on the nature of art *De Pintura Antiga*, written around 1548 and remaining unpublished until the 19th century.

During his long Italian sojourn, before returning to Portugal, the author, then a very young man, had frequented, around 1538, Michelangelo then engaged in the execution of the Last Judgment, within the circle of Vittoria Colonna. In the *Dialogues* he brings in Michelangelo as a character to express his own aesthetic ideas by confronting de Hollanda himself.

The whole treatise, an expression of neo-Platonic aesthetics, is nevertheless dominated by the gigantic figure Michelangelo, as an exemplary figure of the genius artist, solitary and melancholy, invested with a "divine" gift, who "creates" according to metaphysical models, almost in imitation of God. Michelangelo thus became, in De Hollanda's work and in Western culture generally, the first of modern artists.

Discoveries

A 36-cm marble tondo depicting the artist's portrait was first presented in 2005 at the Ideal Museum in Vinci by art historian and critic Alessandro Vezzosi.The work was again presented in 2010 in the Salone del gonfalone of the Panciatichi Palace, seat of the Regional Council of Tuscany during the literary meeting "From Florence to the Stars," curated by Pasquale De Luca.

The work was exhibited in 2011 for a long time at the Caprese Michelangelo Museum in Arezzo.

The work has been cited by James Beck, professor at Columbia University, and is quoted in "Michelangelo Assoluto," Scripta Maneant Edizioni, 2012, edited by Alessandro Vezzosi and introductions by Claudio Strinati.

Physical characteristics

In 2021, paleopathologist Francesco M. Galassi and forensic anthropologist Elena Varotto of the FAPAB

Research Center in Avola, Sicily, examined the shoes and a slipper preserved at Casa Buonarroti, which tradition believes belonged to the Renaissance genius, speculating that the artist was about 5 feet 6 inches tall: a figure in agreement with Vasari, who in his biography of the artist claims that the master was "of medium stature, broad-shouldered, but well proportioned with the whole rest of the body."

Other books by United Library

https://campsite.bio/unitedlibrary